Markings.

Head of Blind-worm. $\frac{1}{2}$

A Book-scorpion (*Chelifer can-croides*). $5/1$

Click-beetle, natural size.

*Sinea diadema*, one of the *Reduviidæ*. (Line shows natural size.)

*a*
Cotton-stainer

*Proxys punctulatus.*

Hellgrammite (*a*) and Hellgrammite-fly.

The Bait-bug.

**Epeiridæ.**
*a*, male, and *b*, female, of *Epeira stellata*; *c*, characteristic orb-web of an epeirid (*Epeira strix*).

Parasite of the Beaver (*Platy-psyllus castoris*). (Line shows natural size.)

Rose-beetle (*Cetonia aurata*). Vertical line shows natural size.

_oderus dorsalis_ (Le Conte). _ line shows natural size.

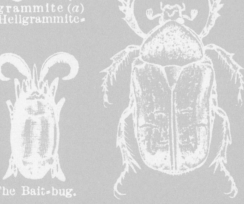

The Twig-gir-dler (*Oncideres cingulata*). $1/1$
*a*, a branch girdled by the beetle.

The Dr Drago (*Dra eatus*)

Hawthorn-tingis _arcuata_), one of the enlarged about ten ti

Flour-beetle (*Te litor*). (Line sho size.)

*Galeruca notata*

WITHDRAWN

W9-CHZ-599

Ground-beetle (*Caloso calidum*), natural size.

*Eurygaster alternatus*; wings partly open. (Line shows natural size.)

A Species of *Phrynus*, about life-size.

Spiderwort Owlet-moth (*Prodenia flavimedia*). *a*, larva; *b*, wings of moth.

Thighed Metapodius (*Metapodius femoratus*).

The Cucujo.

*Ephemeridæ.* European May-fly (*Eph. vulgata*) and its sub-larva.

Bombardier-beetle (*Brachinus stygicornis*). (Vertical line shows natural size.)

*Podisus placidus.* *a*, enlarged; *b*, natural size.

*Libellulidæ.* Development of a dragon-fly, showing the subaquatic larva, emergence from the pupa, and the adult fully winged insect.

A Flea (*Pulex irritans*). *a*, puncturing stylets of the proboscis.

A Bristletail (*Lepisma saccharina*). ⁵/₁

*Phymata erosa.*

*Atypus sulzeri.* (Vertical line shows natural size.)

Bacon-beetle.

Grape-vine Fidia (*F. viticida*). (Line shows natural size.)

# ant

an

t

by

Ting Morris

illustrated by

Desiderio Sanzi

designed by

Deb Miner

A⁺

SMART APPLE MEDIA

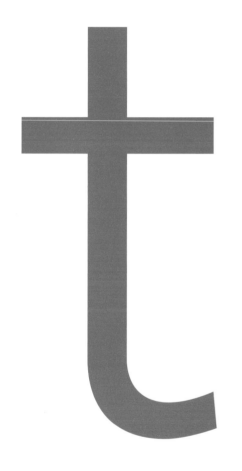

**Who will you meet** on your walk through the woods today?

Listen. Can you hear a rustling sound?

Look. Can you see tiny creatures carrying leaves along the forest floor?

**Turn the page and take a closer look.**

It is just getting light in the forest, and all the plants are covered with dew.

There is a neat stack of pine needles, twigs, and earth piled up in the under-growth. **This is the home of a colony of wood ants.**

But on this chilly spring morning there seems to be no one about. Perhaps the ants are all inside the nest. **Can you see any?**

**THE NEST**

The wood ants' nest is up to 6.5 feet (2 m) high and 13 feet (4 m) across. Around half a million ants usually live in a colony. Some nests have room for up to three million ants.

## OTHER ANT HOMES

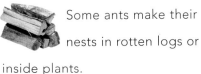 Garden ants feel safe and warm under a large flat stone, concrete slab, or brick.

Some ants make their nests in rotten logs or inside plants.

Weaver ants build tree homes. They stick the edges of two leaves together with silk threads made by their grubs. Each ant builder carries a grub in its jaws and uses it like a tube of glue.

## AN ANT'S BODY

An ant's body has three parts: the HEAD, the trunk (called the THORAX), and the stomach (called the ABDOMEN).

An ant has six legs, with two hooked CLAWS at the end of each one. On each front LEG there are two COMBS. The ant uses these to clean its other legs and its FEELERS (or antennae).

The feelers are used to smell, touch, taste, and hear.

Ants have two EYES, but they can't see very well. Some kinds of ants are blind.

An ant's mouth has strong JAWS for cutting up food, biting enemies, and carrying things.

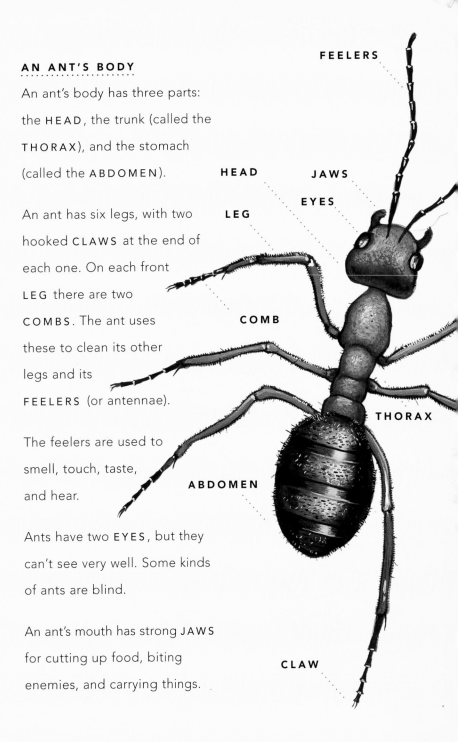

FEELERS

HEAD    JAWS

EYES

LEG

COMB

THORAX

ABDOMEN

CLAW

The queen has informed her nursery ants that she is ready to start laying eggs. She needs more room, more warmth, more air, and more food. The queen likes sweet-tasting foods, and the workers sometimes have to go a long way to satisfy her majesty's demands.

**Can you help this worker feed the queen?** Use your finger to find a way through the maze of tunnels.

### NEST CHAMBERS

Inside the nest there are lots of rooms and tunnels—the queen's chamber, nurseries, rooms for storing food, and even a garbage dump. The ants spend the winter in the deepest underground rooms.

### GETTING THE MESSAGE

Ants talk to each other by making special chemicals that other ants can smell. They give off different smells to tell each other about food, enemies, and nest duties. Ants pick up the scent with their feelers. When two ants tap feelers, they are talking to each other.

Ants from a different colony smell different, so it's easy to recognize outsiders.

GARBAGE DUMP

### BRUSHING UP

Before feeding the queen, worker ants have to clean themselves by brushing off dirt from the outside world.

ROYAL CHAMBER

### ROYAL MESSENGER

The queen stays in contact with all the workers through her nursery ants. She gives out liquid messages on her body, which they lick off of her and pass around the colony.

**A column of ants is marching through the woods in search of food.** Now that the queen's eggs are hatching and the brood is growing, there are many more mouths to feed. News about some exciting food has reached the nest, and workers are on their way to bring it back. **What will they find?** Perhaps some tiny crumbs left behind after a picnic in the woods.

**HELPERS NEEDED**

Ants use teamwork. When an ant comes back to the nest with news about food, it wiggles its feelers, butts heads with other ants, and spits out some of the food it found. Helpers quickly find their way to the food by following a scent trail laid by their fellow workers or by holding on to the leader's hind legs with their feelers. Young ants that can't keep up or get lost along the way are carried by other workers.

### MUSCLE POWER

Ants eat plants, seeds, and other insects. Wood ants sometimes capture wasps and flies. Workers are very strong and can carry things that weigh much more than they do.

### FORAGERS ON THE MOVE

Looking for food outside the nest is a dangerous job. Only older wood ants go on foraging trips. Birds, frogs, and spiders are all enemies, and sometimes ants have to fight with rival ant colonies. People can be a danger too—you might step on an ant without even knowing it.

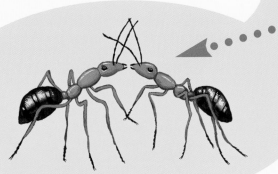

### MOUTH TO MOUTH

Ants carry food by storing it in a special pouch in their stomach called a crop. Then they share it with other ants back in the nest. The feeder passes chewed-up food into the mouth of a hungry ant. If the ant wants more food, it strokes the feeder's head with its feelers.

**13**

**Ants like sweet-tasting food, and this tree is full of goodies.** The wood ants lick the sticky sap from the bark and catch tiny insects that live under it. High up in the branches, they keep their own herds of aphids and milk them like farmers. The ants stroke the aphids and drink the droplets of sweet honeydew that come out of them. This delicious sugary drink is full of vitamins and will later be a special treat for grubs back in the nest.

### ANT GARDENERS

Leaf-cutter ants grow their own food—a large gray fungus. First, workers gather leaves and carry them to the underground "garden" in their nest. There, tiny ant gardeners chew them up and put the pulp on the fungus to make it grow. They weed the garden and have special dumps for their garbage, such as waste and dead ants. All the ants in the colony eat the fungus.

## GOOD FARMERS

Aphids are plant bugs. They suck the sap from plants, and some of this sap comes out of the aphids as sugar. Ants milk aphids by tapping the plant bugs' backs with their feelers. They drink the honeydew and spit it back up to feed the larvae, or grubs, in the nest.

Ants protect aphids from other enemies. They carry them to safety and sometimes even take them into their nest. There they raise them on roots that grow through an underground room.

## NEST GUESTS

Ants often share their nest with other small creatures. Among the lodgers might be wood lice, beetles, spiders, mites, and millipedes. The caterpillar of the blue butterfly is a paying guest. It gives out a sweet liquid that ants love to drink.

Certain tiny ants may build their own nest inside a wood ant home. When the wood ants move to a new area, these squatter ants follow them.

## HONEY POTS

Certain kinds of ants, called honey-pot ants, store liquid food in a special way. They feed their workers with honeydew. The workers then swell up and are used as storage pots for the whole colony. They hang up by their feet in the nest and give out food whenever tapped.

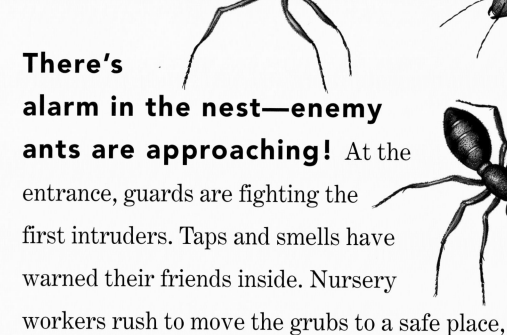

**There's alarm in the nest—enemy ants are approaching!** At the entrance, guards are fighting the first intruders. Taps and smells have warned their friends inside. Nursery workers rush to move the grubs to a safe place, while others go to join the fight.

They grab the enemies' legs and feelers, hold them down, and squirt their deadly poison. The dead ants are dragged away. The wood ants have won the battle and saved their nest.

**ON THE MARCH**

Army ants have very strong jaws. Thousands of ants march in long columns and eat any other insects or spiders they come across.

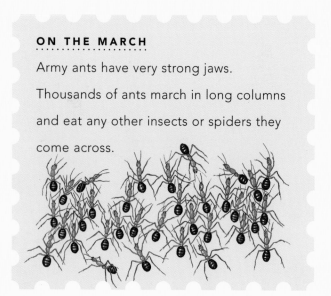

The red garden ant has a nasty sting that is painful to humans. Never pick one up with your fingers.

## ALARM BELLS

When an ant spots an enemy, it goes into a fighting posture and gives off an alarm chemical to warn its nest-mates. During the fight, it makes more alarm smells to call up other fighters.

## BIG HEADS

Some ant colonies have soldiers with big heads, which they use to block the nest entrance. The soldiers open the door only to their own workers with the right smell. Their big heads are also very useful for pushing intruders out of the nest.

## FIGHTING AND BITING

Ants protect themselves by stinging or biting. The poison that comes out of an ant's sharp stinger can kill other insects. A wood ant does not have a stinger but squirts a poison called formic acid. It bites its enemy with its jaws, bends its abdomen between its legs, and squirts poison into the wound.

Feed me! Clean my eggs! Take them to a warm place! Hurry, hurry! These are the queen's orders. **It is hot today, but there's no time for the nursery workers to relax in the sunshine.**

They are busy all the time, licking the newly laid eggs clean and carrying them to warm rooms close to the surface. A few big eggs are taken to a special chamber and given extra helpings of sweet honeydew. These eggs are the future queens.

### SLEEPLESS

Ants never sleep, but they take little rests. Special chambers in a nest are used as resting places for the nursery workers.

### BROTHERS AND SISTERS

The queen lays her eggs in spring and summer. She is the mother of all the ants in the nest. Most of them will be female worker ants, but some will be male ants with wings. A few large eggs get special treatment: nursery workers lick them to pass on honeydew, which feeds the eggs and helps them grow. These lucky few will become winged young queens.

## NURSERIES

There are several nurseries in the nest. Nursery workers keep the eggs warm and clean. If a room becomes too cold or too wet, they move the eggs. If there is a frost, they take the eggs to chambers deep underground.

## ANT EGGS

Eggs that contain worker ants are oval and about half a millimeter in size. Eggs that contain queens are much larger.

## HOW ANTS DEVELOP

Ants go through four stages of development:

### 1 EGG

The eggs are small—about half a millimeter long.

### 2 LARVA

After a few days, the eggs hatch into larvae, or grubs. Nursery ants feed them. When the grubs are about three to five millimeters long, they change again.

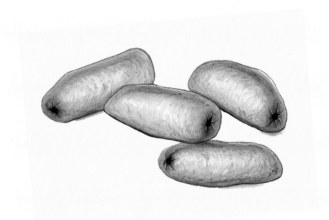

### 3 PUPA

Each larva spins a silk cocoon around itself. Inside the cocoon, it grows into a pupa, or young ant. Nursery ants carry the cocoons up into a sunny spot so they develop more quickly. This stage lasts about three weeks.

**20**

Look what's happening in the nursery. **The baby ants are ready to come out of their cocoons.** But some are too weak to chew their way through. Nursery ants are helping them to struggle free. These pale little ants can't even walk, but in a few weeks' time they will be strong enough to join the workers.

**4 ANT**

When they come out of their cocoons, young ants are pale and cannot walk properly. They are fed and looked after by the nursery ants for another few weeks.

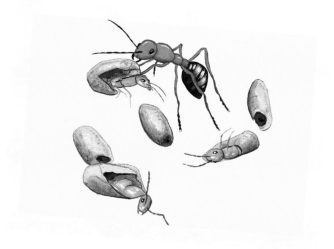

It's a hot, damp summer's day. A young queen is leaving her nest. She spreads her wings and flies high into the sky. Suddenly the air is buzzing with flying ants coming out of the ground. They are male ants from other nests who want to find a queen and mate with her. Today, all the wood ant queens in this forest are on their wedding flight. **Have you ever seen flying ants?**

### A SHORT LIFE

Male ants live only for a few weeks. They can't feed themselves, and they are fed by female workers until their mating flight. After the flight, they are not allowed back into the nest, and they die within a few days.

### BORN WORKERS

A worker's life is hard and dangerous. Workers live for up to five years.

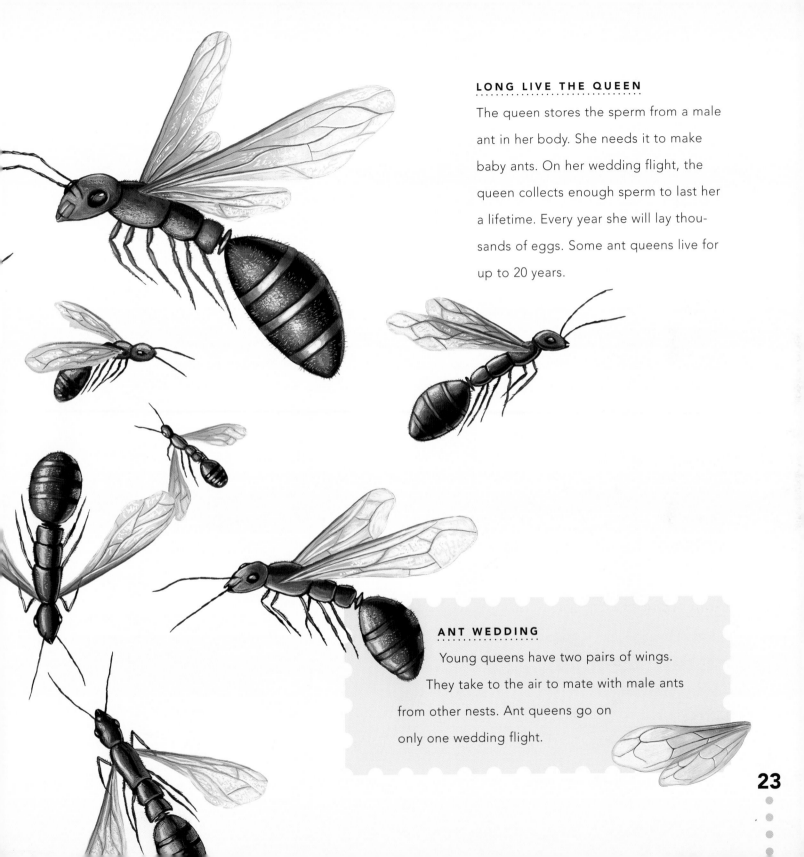

## LONG LIVE THE QUEEN

The queen stores the sperm from a male ant in her body. She needs it to make baby ants. On her wedding flight, the queen collects enough sperm to last her a lifetime. Every year she will lay thousands of eggs. Some ant queens live for up to 20 years.

## ANT WEDDING

Young queens have two pairs of wings. They take to the air to mate with male ants from other nests. Ant queens go on only one wedding flight.

**23**

**A young wood ant queen has landed and is searching for a good nesting site.** She wants a safe, warm place to lay her eggs. Once she finds it, she bites off her wings— she won't need them again— and digs a hole. Then she covers herself up in her small underground chamber. Here the queen will lay her eggs and start a new colony of wood ants.

**HOME SWEET HOME**

Sometimes a young wood ant queen goes back to her old home. Some of the workers build more rooms or move into a new nest with her. All she has to do is lay eggs.

**SLAVE-MAKER**

An Amazon ant queen lays her eggs in another colony's nest. She kills the old queen, and the workers become her slaves and look after her.

24

## NEW COLONY

As the queen has no helpers to look after her, she lives off fat in her own body. When her eggs hatch, she feeds the young grubs herself. But once the first ants are strong enough to help, they do all the work. The queen never leaves the nest again.

Now look back at the picture on page 9. Within a year, the queen's new colony will be crawling with thousands of ants. It will be a big mound with many underground rooms.

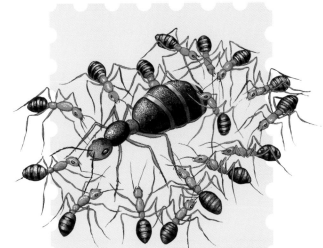

## SOLDIER QUEEN

Army ants don't build a nest, because they are always on the march. When their queen is ready to lay her eggs, the workers simply stop and crowd around her. Within 20 days, the eggs will have grown into young ants ready to march on.

The queen ant
lays eggs.

# Ant

The queen mates
with a male ant.

Most of the ants
become workers.

The eggs hatch into
larvae, or grubs.

The grubs spin
cocoons around
themselves.

# CIRCLE OF LIFE

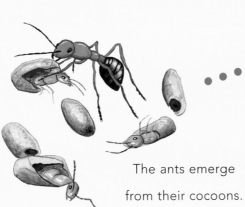

The ants emerge
from their cocoons.

**brood** A large group of babies.

**chamber** A room in a nest.

**cocoons** Silky cases spun by insect larvae, which protect them while they grow into pupae.

**colony** A large group of animals that live close together as a community.

**fertilize** To cause a female insect's eggs to develop into babies.

**foraging** Searching for food.

**fungus** One of a group of very simple living things, such as molds and mushrooms.

**grubs** The young form of some insects; another word for larvae.

**mate** To come together to make babies.

**millipedes** Small creatures with long, thin bodies and many legs.

**mites** Tiny, eight-legged creatures related to spiders.

**nursing** Caring for babies; nursery ants take care of baby ants.

**sap** The juice inside a plant that serves as its food.

**sperm** Fluid produced by male animals that makes a female's eggs grow into babies.

**squatter** An animal that lives in another animal's nest.

**vitamins** Substances found in food that are needed by animals for good health.

**wedding flight** A flight made by winged queen ants when they mate with male ants.

Published by Smart Apple Media

1980 Lookout Drive

North Mankato, Minnesota 56003

Copyright © 2005 Smart Apple Media.
International copyrights reserved in all
countries. No part of this book may be
reproduced in any form without written
permission from the publisher.

Illustration: Desiderio Sanzi

Design: Deb Miner

**Library of Congress
Cataloging-in-Publication Data**

Morris, Ting.
Ant / by Ting Morris.
p. cm. — (Creepy crawly world)
Summary: An introduction to the physical
characteristics, behavior, and life cycle of ants.
ISBN 1-58340-376-0
1. Ants—Juvenile literature.
[1. Ants] I. Title.

QL568.F7M67 2003
595.79'6—dc21   2002042793

Head of Blind-worm. $1/2$

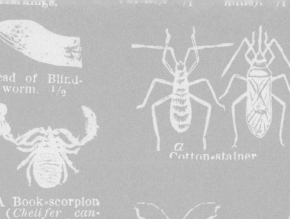

A Book-scorpion (*Chelifer cancroides*). $5/1$

$a$, Cotton-stainer

*Epeiridæ.*

$a$, male, and $b$, female, of *Epeira stellata*; $c$, characteristic orb-web of an epeirid (*Epeira strix*).

*Proxys punctulatus.*

Click-beetle, natural size.

Hellgrammite ($a$) and Hellgrammite-fly.

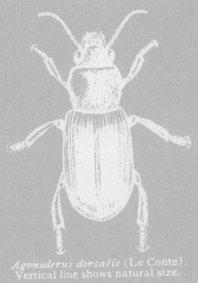

Parasite of the Beaver (*Platypsyllus castoris*). (Line shows natural size.)

*Agonoderus dorsalis* (Le Conte). Vertical line shows natural size.

The Twig-girdler (*Oncideres cingulata*). $1/1$

$a$, a branch girdled by the beetle.

The Dr
Dragon
(*Drac
eatus*)

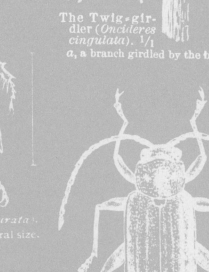

Hawthorn-tingis
*arcuata*), one of the
enlarged about ten ti

*Sinea diadema*, one of the *Reduviidæ*. (Line shows natural size.)

The Bait-bug.

Rose-beetle (*Cetonia aurata*). Vertical line shows natural size.

Flour-beetle (*Te
litor*). (Line show
size.)

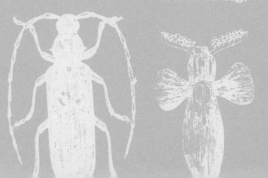

*Galeruca notata*

Ground-beetle (*Caloso calidum*), natural size.

*Ephemeridæ.* European May-fly (*Eph. vulgata*) and its sub-larva.

*Phymata erosa.*

*Eurygaster alternatus*; wings partly open. (Line shows natural size.)

Bombardier-beetle (*Brachinus stygicornis*). (Vertical line shows natural size.)

*Atypus sulzeri.* (Vertical line shows natural size.)

A Species of *Phrynus*, about life-size.

Thighed Metapodius (*Metapodius femoratus*).

*Libellulidæ.* Development of a dragon-fly, showing the subaquatic larva, emergence from the pupa, and the adult fully winged insect.

Spiderwort Owlet-moth (*Prodenia flavimedia*). *a*, larva; *b*, wings of moth.

The Cucujo.

*Podisus placidus.* *a*, enlarged; *b*, natural size.

A Flea (*Pulex irritans*). *a*, puncturing stylets of the proboscis.

Grape-vine Fidia (*F. viticida*). (Line shows natural size.)

A Bristletail (*Lepisma saccharina*). 5/1

Bacon-beetle.

One o